MW01016932

Songs for my Father

Katherine Lazaruk

 FriesenPress

One Printers Way
Altona, MB R0G 0B0
Canada

www.friesenpress.com

Anita Alberto Photography
www.anitaalberto.com

ISBN
978-1-03-915975-4 (Hardcover)
978-1-03-915974-7 (Paperback)
978-1-03-915976-1 (eBook)

1. POETRY, CANADIAN

Distributed to the trade by The Ingram Book Company

Contents

Whatever other truth lay in the unlitigated unmitigated past between us,

the confrontation of the unvarnished truth would be an offering worthy of the name.

And besides, at least he'll know how I felt.

If he reads it.

All I desired

All I desired,
really,
was for
him
(dadfathermanallmen)
to want me.

Dads should want their kids, right?

Their daughters?

To guide, protect,
steer clear of the dangers
of menallmenandtheworld
because they know, they know
what men can be,
the world
the beasts
inside, outside, around,
but
he
didn't
couldn't
wouldn't
face his own beasts enough
to spend any time
helping me tame mine, and
I listen to all the songs
those other women write,
all the words describing
their good fathers and I,

I
I can't
I can't write
I can't write that.

What could he say?
"You're right, I didn't" or
"You're wrong, I did" or
"Here's what I learned" or
"I'm sorry that I wasn't ready" or
"I never knew how to show you" or

"I was scared" or

"I was barely more than a kid myself" or . . .

What?

The trouble with family

The trouble with family is
everyone has an opinion,
but only some opinions are
okay to have, and
unfortunately,
sadly,
ouch!
These opinions can bite.
Loyalty looking like love,
fear, ferocious, fealty
sworn duty deafening!

Makes minute the dissenting

opinion: I'm pretty sure love

isn't supposed to feel
like this.

I am not the victim here

I've slung my fair share of
shit over the years but
I'd put all my handfuls down
in an instant

if

I weren't so busy
defending myself.

I used to think

I used to think
that family (patriarchy) meant
unquestioning loyalty and
maybe it does, but
does it
mean I have to make room
for those who continue
to treat me
indifferently?
Coldly?
Badly?

No ... yes ... maybe ... no ... ?

It's best to know the

It's best to know the
history so there's no
mystery, no
lies, but
beware, you might
just find what
you're looking for and
fuck, man, this is
(likely)
going to hurt and
we all know how
we go mad at that.

I confess

I confess
I love
to sing.
I confess
I love
to be loved, to love and
I confess that my offer,
unoffered,

might

be

shit, but

at least
there's compost
in the end, to grow.

I confess that my
artmusicwriting
is my lifeline,
preserver, hook
linesinkersought
I wishwantneed
to confess.

The heart of me,
opened opens opined,
notes hit sweetly!
Lines pulled long,
the rests,
the rest, the
life of me rests
in music and it,

It

It is
It is
It is
It is not
It is not

Not

Mere

Expression

But

Existence.

Deep soul stirs!
Spaces, bars!
Staves, staged!
Staved off attacks, and
in all things it
held me
artful,
soothed and
adagio andante,
lullaby
lullaby, and

I confess

I'm still
just a child,
new
in this place,
insideoutin,

(littlebabylullay)

a child.

I wish I had had

I wish I had had a
gentle guiding hand, a
voice for my voice,
before I had my own,
solid,
to help me learn sooner
to choose, not be chosen for,
and a heart to hear me,
give the me the right thing
to grow to sing to be
to growl, grope, ground, and
grapple with
all the beasts, besting and bested.

Mine!

I needed someoneanyone

I needed someoneanyone.

You, fathermotherbrotherfamilytree,

to tell me all the little things
you noticed and valued, to be

reflective,
true,

so I might see
myself into myself and
from that place, that precioussacredplace

shine,

mirrored moonlakeoceanskies,
sail, salt giving outoverbackskim
in boat oat throat,
sheets to the wind, winding!
Sing me out and out and out, over!
Skyward bound, stars, start, set me up,

up!

Set me up.

Set me up.

It's painful to

be around you

and pretend your

mirrors

didn't come

from the funhouse.

My brother learned

My brother learned
his lessons well
at my father's feet.
Tossing grenades
and running.

Jealousy

Jealousy:

Feeling or showing envy of
my brother's achievements and
advantages.

My brother

My brother,
all of his ease,
(diseasedisseddistant)
jock popularity humour
cutting edges clipped
in interactions with me and
no way in, into him, for me, wanting.

We, impersonal,
living in the same house,
under the same roof,
under the same
abuser (to me),
Dad (to him).
His easy connection with
hockeygolfsports and coaching,
lawn-mowing, outdoor work, and cars
and all the affection my mother described
for him, the firstborn, the son.
The times she remembered when they would
sit together, babydad, skin to skin and she knew
not to (wouldn't) talk to them
until they started talking to each other,
in the mornings, in the trailer
where we lived, at first.

He picked up the scapegoat energy
and poured it out on me, namecalling,
putting me in the goal just to shoot at me,
in my hockey-net desperation to be
connected, just connected,

to someone who might be (but wasn't)
having a similar experience.
I was jealous of my brother, oh sure,
he got his share of yelling but
he never seemed to mind,
could successfully, like my mother,
turtle up and let it roll
off his back, off his shell.
Able to pick the battles, not many,
and mostly avoid the ring,
when all I wanted to do was
stop the fight entirely,
unsure of why
a fight existed at all in a place
(homefamilyspace)
that should be the last for fighting

(or at least should be for fighting fair).

Why am I the target?

I was blessed

I was blessed
(and not blessed)
with the sound of music.

My voice,
all voice, voices,
loud and long
raw, and wriggling, ornery, rough!

Untempered, temper
tantrum, rage!

(at the start)

But
with time,
with temperance,
with training and technique,
and tears
(so many)

I was blessed with and
stretched with and given
more range, more,
more intonation in tune,
tuning,
harmonizing, and
reading.

Sight unseen, learning,
emerging and
seen, just a little
by the first choir teacher
to help me see that standards,

(boundaries?)

standards were good things to have.

Anchors are a

Anchors are a
weight drag drop,
holding down,
slowing up,
steadying, directing,
pacing, and
sometimes they
hold you back
when they should be
holding fast.

Anchored in.
Anchored on.
Anchored with.

Ancora, ancora,
again and again,
returning to
the safety of
breath, notes.

Adagio, andante, allegro,
supported.

Adapted, angular,
vocal and not,
verbal and not,
words and words,
and tunes and not,
with family but
notable and
music, muse

was mine,

tenacious.

Gradually, she invited me

Gradually, she (teachermotherauntiewoman)
invited me,
ten, young and trying,
conducted, taught
(molded) me in,
into the musical world, inhabited
with other voices and my own,

Acknowledged.

Found me things that
worked for me and for my voice
and handled me gently enough that
I could cry if it wasn't working,
cry myself through to the end, push
(a little)
(gentle)
(kindnessalwayswins).

The Sound of Music was one of the first
(the hills are alive you know),
a comfortable key, a costume
a stage presence and joy in the song,
sense of confidence from winning the
two-foot-tall trophy for junior musical theater
in one of the anymany competitions I won
as a moderately talented kid, a hard worker,

(desperate)
(take that, brother)
(but)

at home no place for my trophy,

(or me, it seemed),

amidst all the hockey and golf trophies
of my brother so I,

I created
I created a
I created a shrine
I created a shrine to
I created a shrine to myself

Pictures up the wall, trophies on the shelf,
looking up from my bedroom's desk,
trying to remember who I was

before
I got here.

Homesick,

heartsick,

lonely,

unloved.

He was so mad

He was so mad,
my father,
always, and I
thought maybe
it was (of course)
my fault.

Was it?

When he didn't
dealwithfaceup and
pace through
his own monsters,
they became
belonged
lived
moved in
with
me,
lodged in that
secretpainfulplace,
stinging, a thousand
paper cuts of
cutting remarks,
voices that
stopped me.
From living.
From singing.
From sound.

Or, at least,
they tried.

She said I was good

She said I was good, (teachermotherauntiewoman).
Not in so many words but
in opportunity extended,
in the exasperated patience
of notes that cracked and clipped
my wings as I learned to fly
out on the limbs of lips and tongue,
teeth and vocal folds,
folded into shapes and sounds,
vibrating me out, one crack at a time.
Handing me new things to try,
giving me a taste of what it might mean to
find my voice, my place, my
rightful entitlement to use all the
breath in me to breathe,
in and out, in, and, out . . . in . . . and . . . out,
to craft lines of beauty and to
understand the value
of a pause.

She said I was good, (teachermotherauntiewoman),
affirmed me and more,

she actually liked me,

I think.

I've always been chasing

I've always been chasing,
my entire life, lived, lied
Chasing the love,

(fatherbrother)
(all men,any)
(musicGodchurchspirit)
(searching)
(searching)
(soul)

in the midst of the fear of men,
I'm chasing, chasing,
choosingcatching,
catching glimpses of
(loveofmusic)
(acceptanceconnectionapproval),
the rabbit's tail
just out of my
hounding mouth,
around around around
corners, cornered,
waiting, just waiting for them to turn
to me, not on me,
as they did, do, will again,
cursing, chafing, cold, cruel and
it's so confusing when men
who say they love you

do things that hurt you
and laugh, then
kick your trophies, your tunes,
your voice and choice all
down, down deep and then
say, backtracking fakery,

"Don't take it all so personally!"

You're too sensitive,
it's just a joke.

Can't you take it?

Take it?
             Take it!

Take it.

                              Ugh.

Say something good

Say something good
Give me . . . something . . .

good.

Family is (or should be)

Family is (or should be)
the safe place,
the warm place,
the best place to be
secure, to be free.
Unleashing your grace
and face on the world,
catapulting you from
a bed of loveacceptanceappreciation
into the full heightsanddepths
wide range of life, ranging
far and far, further,
secure in heart and soul!
A family who cares deeply
cares greatly and well,
invests the timeenergy, all
in loving fiercely,
in safety, safely,
comforting me,
foundational me,
Strongsteadystable,
be there for me,
ride or die loyalty,
pull together and
see
one another for
all their joyfulsorrowful parts,

And love.
And love.
And love.

But . . .

I felt
that love was a lot to ask,

all signs point here . . .
I am a burden, heavy

#impact

And yes,

I'm too sensitive

for this.

I just don't

think you get it,

don't get

me

and

worse,

you barely

even tried.

The intermediary

The intermediary,
mother, mymother,
Styx ferryboatman, mainline,
shuttling between shores,
the darkness of him and
the terror of me.

Connected,
disconnected,
ferried secondhand messages,
triangulating tense terror,
trying to sootheplacatemanage,

all his emotional labour
heavy in her boat.

You might drown, when
You first start to swim, but

It's okay . . .

You murder the life you're living to
get the life you want.

A mother's love

A mother's love
can only do so much
when cloaked
in a father's indifference.

He did set me up

He did set me up,
(myfathermybrother)
beautifully but,
not the way he
might have meantwanted to, but
unconscious impact,
unwarranted, unknown,
left traces,

whether he meant to or not.

I didn'tdon't show you

I didn'tdon't show you
all the tender parts
of me, anymore.

I didn'tdon't show you
My art, my heart.

I didn't show you, don't
who I amwas anymore because
I didn'tdon't want your judgement.

So if you think
you knewknow me,
trust me
you didn'tdon't, but

He did.

He took me

He took me
(my teacher)
(him new, at school)
at face value, I
young, fourteen, and
groomed all my messy parts
into a semblance of
the lover he wished he could have,
at twenty-five.

(teacherteachingtaught)

He waited . . . dropping,

dropping his
(loving?)
words, looks, cards, letters, notes
on me, gentle rain,
gradually, pooling in the
dark coves and dips, my
soothingheatsoft, heart
(unknown)
with what felt like a
(miraculous)
warmth to the fatherfamily's
indifferentcold and
filled vacancyvoid,
validation, velvety, soft.

He didn't touch me then but
waiting,
speaking,
looking,
whispering
special somethings,
waiting,
until I, aged into
consent, theoretically,
consented to
his what looked like love, and
paid his price for all that
should have been at
home for free, homefree and
affirmation for me was
a powerful drug and
under his hands
I learned what I thought
you, my father, maybe
always thought
I was for.

So mature for my age,
father confused me,
an early reader of adult words,
romance bodice ripper, porn,
mixed messages,
stimuli with shame, simultaneous
be sexy but not a slut, dirtyenticing, but clean
naughtyfunny be hiddensecret and show but
not like that, short skirts, tight pants.
I didn't understand why I could read it,
conspiratorially, but not be it?
Taught me to pour the perfect beer,
massage his neck and shoulders, surrogate wife maybe, ew?
Warped connection, tightly woven libido learning, weird,
this is what men want and how women should be,
but no, not like that, shamed, mybodymindselfsoulsick, wanting,
desire developing, am I pretty?
What I thought I knew, fifteen.
The teacher touched me then and I thought, rebelteendefiant,
Daddy, are you proud of me now?

Why do we always blame

Why do we always blame
the daughter for
daddy issues when
it's clear that the
issues are usually his?

Through storm, high dry winds
of my masculine
dead-prairie existence,
nothing grows if you never water it
and I asked my father,

(in my mind, never aloud, allowed)

"When will you ever stop salting my earth?"

And still

And still,
I sang.
Quietly, chorally,
solos and duets, trios and all that
harmony, leaning on my sight-reading friends
and amplifying their correct chords,
notes and notes and notes and
that
is what kept me
alive.

Did you know?

The only reason
I didn't kill myself
was because
I didn't want to
make a mess.

And then, she left

And then, she left
they left, lifted
(teachermotherauntiewoman)
turned me over to lift life,
to what she (they) thought was
next-level learning, school,
more school and I,
I excited,
leaned in and left too but
didn't miss, don't, but it,
it wasn't,
I wasn't,
it wasn't . . .

It wasn't until the

It wasn't until the
absence of women,
gentle,
that I trippedturned
tracked rightwrongly
into the old white guys' trap!

(We know what's best for you)

not pulling me out from myself,
what I knowknewnow is
best for me, like women knew,
gentle, exploratory, kind,
seeing me and sensing into
all the corners of my mind,
all the expression of my heart,
and
no one gets to tell you
what your artist
has to say, but man,
those men sure try.

Is this what the witches felt like before they burned?

#metoo

Am I allowed?

Am I allowed to
rewrite, renown, owned on the
bookpagepaper
already done?

I'm scared to confess
how deeply what meaning
music (family) sits in me, situates
moves me, in out and up and
how I feel because
the risk of
walking around
broken wide open is
too much to bear.

Can the page even carry this, or
will it be house of cards tumbling,
nothing?

I'm afraid it's nothing,
and all that they (he) said was
true,
that there's no place for me
onstage, this stage, staged,
family show or for audience
external
performing, singsongsinging,
awful.

Am I?
Awful?

I might be awful.

I don't think I'm awful but damn,
this doubt!
Am I willing to have it be
awful?

Shit?

Shit.

I need to remember this

I need to remember this:

It's never me.
It's always the song.

I hate this fucking song

I hate this fucking song
(BattiBatti, bullshitMozartaria)

but I didn't know enough then,
(collegeuniversitygoingpro)

only knowing now
that I couldcan choose
my
art,
that my heart would
always know
what was right
or not
for me, or not, and
Batti, batti
(bullshitMozartaria)
was a perfect reflection of
what he
(oldwhitemananotherteacher grr)
wanted me to be,
envisioning himself as the
Don Giovanni of the Voice Faculty
and I, one of his many Zerlinas,
hopeful he, always,
that one of us would
submit
to his greasypoorme wanderings
and his reminiscing
of a time when
he played
(a few minor roles)
in New York.

"You have a beautiful oral cavity,"

he said,

"I bet you could do beautiful things
With your beautiful oral cavity."

He winked at me then, with that
grosscapering grin, bearded, old and
unkempt, sure in his path and his
cultish ways, pedagogical promises
laid out step by step to those
young women like me who
didn't know any better.

He asked us to babysit, errands and such,
wormingworkingweaving his way in,
told us stories of his wifely woes and how
he was the only one
who really knew
how it was
to be a professional opera singer,
from his weird washed-up shores of
Vancouver, smalltownsmalltime
too big for its britches,
all those who refused him,

bitches.

So he assigned arias,
(avenging his wounded ego)
not for me, for us, but
for him, gratified

as we ground down
on the edges of songs
not meant for our voices, only
stereotypes of sopranos,
mediocres of mezzos,
assortments of altos,
ablation by adagio, removing us
from our artists, piece by piece, ourselves
hourly, recitaled, wrecked and

Fach!

He was bad for women, but
no one said a word because
you know,
he wasn't the worst.

I'm sorrynotsorry, still not

I'm sorrynotsorry,
still not sorry,
resistant,
wrangling with sorry
ass situations where
somewhere I
sat and thought of
all the sorry words
that were said,
never acknowledged,
and I apologize
(tomemyself)
for forgetting
you were

a dick.

Dicks drove my bus

Dicks drove my bus, as soon as they could
we women, pussies hidden, secret makings
vulvar volume muted as the dicks yelled and
straightened and strutted their hard up hard time
stuff, coming up and out, all over my face
just to keep driving my bus, my bus
some drove with pain, others with
pleasure hiding the pain inherent in
control and coercion, gentle and sweet
while on the flipside, see-side, shame.
The women, guerilla warfare for me but
ineffective in the big picture because
here I am, still trying to find my way
out, thirty-six years later.
Winding out from transit directions,
there's no app for this and why, oh why
did I let them drive my bus, my bus?
Is it only because they told me they knew better,
or never told me anything at all, or
only told me what I needed to hear so
I'd sing my songs for them, or for them to force
their songsideasbeliefs of what it meant to be
a singer, on me?

Where did my voice go when it got off the bus?

What fired me up, finally

What fired me up, finally
opened eyes wide, therapeutic journey healing,
what opened the door to see monsters made flesh
was way back when, on visiting my hometown,
intermission at the symphony,
I saw him (fifteentwentysixteacherabuser)
in the doorway, leaning into her ear.
A pretty young thing, much younger than him
and I thought, "Fuck," he's doing it again.
(teacherteachingtaught) and

THE RAGE!
THE RAGE ROSE!

In my throat, my song at last, a fierce
PROTECTIVE rage burning!
Burned down his reputation
and mine, then,

police unbelieving,
family shaming and
angry, so angry
at me, not him, sadly.
Shamed me, ashamed of me, blamed and,
no law to fix me, slipped through the loopholes legally.

He moved away because they watched him closely,
his teaching certificate suspended and now he's off
teaching private students who knows what shitty games,
predatory fuck.

That's the thing about beauty without power, self-knowledge.

You'll take any kind of soft feedback, soft mouth, soft touch,
not seeing the hidden teeth,

jagged and broken and ready to tear you up, gross,
and only my friend, even keel,
seeing me crack and crawl said
that's what stress leave is for,
permission to be broken and okay and then
my counsellor, wise
woman, safe said,

(forthefirsttime)
(Iheard)

It's not your fault,

and

I

wept.

I abandoned myself

I abandoned myself.
I, abandoned, myself.
Abandoned I, myself.

Myself.
Myself.

Abandoned, I abandoned.
Myself.

I sacrificed myvoicemyself
just a little but a lot
on the altar, altering me
to be
just a little
to try
just a little
just a little
just a little,
quiet, not quite but
quit, playing songs I knew,
not growing into ones I didn't,
safe in familiarity and away from
abuse of my artist, safe, as long as
I played what I already knew.
Practicing isn't supposed to sound good,
that's why we practice, and we don't
sing for an audience until we sing for ourselves

and I
abandoned
myself

singing
for
myself.

Instead,

I
sang
for
you, and

you

throttled

me.

Sometimes I think I need
a resurrection,

restoration
letting his wounds
be his
allhisallmen

not my fault,
not about me.

No.

#therapysucks

I began to dig

I began to dig
deeper, into the past,
dark soil, soiled,
pulled out all the
dark corners and
investigated,
invested in myself to
remember.

The first time I ran away

The first time I ran away
I was three,
and that should tell you
all you need to know about
how I felt about the fit
of my family for me, but
it's more complicated
than that, because
I have this idea, you see,
of what a family should be and
I keep falling in love
with it, overandoveragain,
and sure, they did the bare minimum
for parental provision so
I always had
food
shelter
clothing
education
activities
and I'm grateful for that
but
love
was
MIA,
in a way, and sure,

it's a #firstworldproblem
when kids grow up in the barrens,
emotional wilderness affection deserts
stretching out long,
sensing something is wrong
before you even know
what love is or is supposed to be.
Nothing can change the past, no,
but acknowledging harm helps.

When your father is twelve

When your father is twelve,
or maybe five,
emotionally speaking,
stagnantstuckyuck,
you don't get to be twelve
or five.

Instead, you grow up quickly,
eggshelling your way through
his fits and starts of
terrifying temper
that blow through your world,
destroy your joy,
your childhood, your naivete,
your fivetwelvegrowth
stunted by giant feet,
stomped on your heart,
gestating rage in you,
growing hate of self,
judgement and criticism,
never ending bile,
a pile of excrementdefecating
on your head until you're covered in

All
His
Shit.

I even had to find my own shovel.

People, flower parents
Who don't lovewant
orchid kids, but have them
couldmightmaybeperhapsoughto
pick up a gardening manual?

Love is where the good families live

Love is where the good families live,
but mine moved firmly into
obligation and debt,
deficits of defaulting
loans, not gifts, grudgingly given.

Never free, not easy, and never,

ever (okay, maybe once or twice)

kind.

It's a low bar
and mine taught me early
not to ask.

Once I asked my brother

Once I asked my brother,
"Hey, do you think we should try harder
to be friends?"
and he said,
"Why would I be your friend?"

If we hadn't grown up
in the same house,
he reasoned,
we wouldn't even know
each other, we
have nothing in common
and though that's probably true,
it hurts to hear
you aren't worth it
to your brother, so instead,
two casual, too casual
acquaintances casually
meeting over the back of
the elephant in the room,
my perspectiveexperienceincidence
too confronting
to confront.

"Are you crazy? Our childhood was great."

(!!!)

It's amazing to me how
one sibling can see
it all so differently.

"They did the best they could."

We lived in two
different families but
it wasn't our parents
who were divorced.

You need space and time to

You need space and time to
practice, make perfect and
it's a practice, practice is.

Room.

I asked my uncle

I asked my uncle
what he remembered about
my father in their youth and
he said,
"He got the worst of it because
he never knew when to shut up."

I asked my cousins what they
thoughtfeltfeel about their fathers,
my uncles,
the gruff men, grumpy and brusque,
they all had a temper but

not
one

not one cousin told me
that they were

afraid.

Afraid

Afraid of

Afraid of their

Afraid of their father.

Fuck!

My cousins were (are) great

My cousins were (are) great,
all that family should be.
Loyal,
caring,
watching from afar,
affirming, confirming
that maybe I wasn't so
crazy, and
yes,
my dad
was abusive.

My aunties

My aunties,
onetwoorthree or more,
each side,
loved me then,
love me still.
Oblique references,
coded bitsbytes,
Javaspeak before programmed,
rogue,
their wordsquestions questioning,
asking if I was okay,
knowing I was not
and yet, the sense, felt sense of
their love
helped, abitalittlealot and
sustaining,
kept my tiny "I am" flame

Alive.

Somewhere between the

Somewhere between the
family, therapy, unraveling,
and the music, raveled,
twotiedtogethertoo.
I lost, I found, I grew angry,
grew myself, spectrum,
volume vocabulary, emotional
and, singing, practiced.
Emotional, what? Practice.
Notes, what? Practice.
Practice practice practice
of speaking, of song,
lifelong longing
connecting all the unconnected
unconvinced, dots
on page, spots, spotting
myself, hidden, unhidden,
hides and all the songs I sang
contained my father within
and all the desire for him
to say too,

I was good.

Enough.

Practice rooms only help you

Practice rooms only help you
be small in small spaces

fitting in thousands of hopefuls
notes and notes, but notes
and hopefuls need
room!

But . . .

Smothered, still, squandered
notes of nothing, dropping
six inches from your face,
not sailing out and over
to the backs of halls made,
purposeful, purposely,
purported to contain

the voice,

for real.

Not muzzled or muted.

After all, we're not trumpets.

Gross green aged carpet
Orange seventies fabric walls
Silenced, soundproofed
Old pianos sticky with keys

How does anyone grow in a
vacuum pack?

far can you go, out on
kinny branch?

can you go, out on the skinny branch?
ng broadly, bell-like, brooms to fly on
e confines of composers long dead
hey'd be horrified to see
ir work has become, preserved
d, pruned and protected, and
grees, as they're structured now,
hing but notes on notes of
d, nevergrow, neverthink,
ules, learn the ways and
don't,

ide the lines.
 colours, no scribbling!
xcept the acceptable,

es, one to the other
he silos!
g to no one,
ng out solo,

I have a brother (no brother)

I have a brother (no brother).
I have a father (no father).
I have teachers (no teachers).
All men.
All absent.
From me and
(I'm) fine (not fine)
with it
(it seems), but
better to be
absent
than
presently
reinjuring me
regularly,
rejecting my
being
doing
having.
The music of me,
tuneless discordant
to them, it seems,
but then, they never were
music lovers.

How
the s

How fa
Branchi
out of th
I think tl
what the
performe
music de
mean not
nevermin
learn the r
absolutely
don't dare
to move
to colour
to grow
inside, outs
Only certai
No drama,
jostling
jouncing
jousting,
knights' lanc
and silos, all
Singers singi
pianists hang
brass players,
strings,

percussion in the basement,
theory separate from practice,
sightsinging separate from song,
and nothing on the story of
anything you were learning.
Music degrees just meant
you spent four years in class, but
what did you really learn
in school?

athome

in life

longlearning

what?

I owe

I owe
I owe nothing
I owe nothing to
I owe nothing to anyone.

But

But
(and)
the worst part is
I don't know why
he didn't like me.

Creeplingsneakyvoices

Creeplingsneakyvoices,
trying to convince me
it wasn't true, I was wrong.

Making me doubt

Making me doubt
my
experience

is
worse

than

my experience,
I think.

The nice thing

The nice thing
isn't proof
that the bad thing
didn't happen.

I wish this story

I wish this story
would have a happy ending,
but then
we never talk
about that.

A hope

A hope
not based in truth
is delusion.
The hope of a child,
without evidence,
false, and
abandonment
of the same
is true,
without penance,
contrition acknowledgement,
bare base level.
It's not the child's job
to make the parent
love them,
at five or fifty.
The power of a parent
is constant and
requires responsible exercise,
and I'm tired of
completing their assignments.

Dad is an earned title

Dad is an earned title,
earned slowlyalways,
through dayssecondsyears,
moments, developmental,
developing care and carefully
sharing themselves and the world
with the children they shepherd
into the wolf's mouth, dark and
sunshine light.
Training wheels, crawlwalkrunning
with, not against,
standing before, behind, beside, and
up for their dear and
see, hear, affirm,
before gentle teaching, correcting.

"That's my daughtersonnonbinarythemthey!"
they say, proud, proudly, loudly,
laying claim to while claiming not,
leaving choice and voice and grace to
their children to growknowlearn.
Never cruel,
accepting always and
helping parse and splice and dice all the
tiny little bits of life, lessoned, learning.

There's more and more,
but good dads don't fail
or, if faltering,
find a way to take their own shortcomings
and use them as a way into showing
their children that they too, are learning,
growing,
changing,
loving,
laughing.
See, see,
hear, hear,
affirm, affirm.

Nobody's perfect, but
good dads might be close.

I read once that

I read once that
it's not that kids are hurt
by trauma,
but that they are

alone

with the hurt,
and it rang a bell.

(severalallclangingdingdongshrill)

It wasn't what happened,
but how it happened to me,
and the aftermath.

They didn'tknowdon'tknow
that I wasamalone
with the hurt.

These are the songs for my father

These are the songs for my father,
all the songs
I have written in my heart.

For all the times

For all the times
he held me hostage
$$$$$ooooooooothed
under his moneyfinancialterrorism
(his golden rule)
"He whohasthegoldmakestherules,"
he said, and
he's right.
That worldly view,
(patriarchalfuckery)
is true, but
I have my own gold now,
thank God, and
I've been banking his
shadows, stinky slinking, and
soon I'll be lighting my
matches to

burn
it
all
down,

light it all up and
banish the last
of the past,
of him, from me so
I can move again.
Breathe.
Exhale.

I used to sing, you know

I used to sing, you know.
Sang, loved to sing, took
joy in my songs and
felt whole, sometimes, and I,

I was
I was good,
or at least,
good enough, but
my father was
jealous, I think.

Every chance he could take, to
coil his lusty green snake around
my throat, constricting vibration and squeeze?

He took.
(i fought)
He took.
(i fought)

Before he throat-fucked me with his rage
(energetically)
(not physically, ew)
(that's gross and worse)
(but)
stuffed my words down into my gut,
(swallowedchokedunspoked)
he murdered me with his own wounds.

I used to sing, you know,
Weighted by the judgments of
men who claimed to be
teaching me a lesson
about my beautiful oral cavity doing
beautiful things.
Oh, I could sing but
I could also suck a dick,
my beautiful mouth and lips busy
with their pleasures and
not my songs and that

That is
That is a
That is a high
That is a high price to
That is a high price to pay

for some small
affirmationconfirmationlove
of my voice, of me.

My voice
IS
me.

I'm going

I'm going
I'm going to
I'm going to find
I'm going to find my
I'm going to find my real
I'm going to find my real voice.

(it's gone, abducted)

The violence of vanishing
these songs are lovely bones,
a graveyard, digging,
Golden Compass severing of soul
slowly, one note, one measure, one piece
at a time, but vanished still.

Now a quest for questions, quickly!
Query:
If I hadn't let the dicks on the bus
where might I have gone?

Let's find out, explore, implore!
Tread, retread, the roads untaken!
My life is too short for silence, but . . .

I'm terrified to meet my voice and

I'm terrified to meet my voice and
aching to meet her but
even as I climb this long hill to get there
I can feel it tightening in my chest
breathless, breathing bated,
threatening to choke me or perhaps that's
just the feeling of the dam
damming me, holding back the waterairfireearth,
always, often, never again, never, but trying,
trying to fuck me into submission and
as I stand at the top of the hill
at the bottom of the stairs,
facing yet another climb,
this personal Everest search for
my true voice,
my true terror
rises up, extant and
who or what will become of me
if I unleashunveilunlock this
dragon's breath?

Will I ever stop screaming?

In their caverns, thosemen

In their caverns, thosemen,
I looked for the father that
might have been
if he had spent more time
strangling his own demons
instead
of creating mine.
I used to sing, you know.

Now, I sing just a little,
quietly, not full throated, not often,
the gremlin around the corner
on my shoulder
stops me with judgement.
Does thisthat sound good?
(doyoulikemelikemedoyou?)
Or not?
(is this singing safe?)

Oh no,
blow all the hatred out vocally
changeflyflow
trauma head to toe,
sticking me with flint or
cold analysis
kills that emergentflameart.

It's so dangerous to comment but
my gremlins have comments,
constant, and to
shut them up
requires more than I've got
sometimes and
therapeutic volume
volumizes my pain, my joy,
a wall of wailing and I am made sound,
waving whole, just a little, but
I am loud and I can't . . .

I can't . . .

When someone is listening
it changes things.
Witnessing is witnessing but
watching and listening,
different.

I think I can't sing.

I can sing.

I can't sing.

(can'tbreathe)

I can can't can

Can't

Can

Fucking want to, love the effort
effortless,
a full-throated holler
down the holler feels real
and crushed at the same time.
sometimes by
my father's voice and
their voices and

(his voice, mine now? no)

weighted, waiting, heavy

(they really don't get emergence, protective, do they?)

and there's no place right
(rightnowright)
for me to be loud but here
(rightnowwrite).

Writing is so
quiet and so

I speak.

Aloud.

In singing these old

In singing these old,
significant songs, pivotalpast
assigned for good or ill,
first of their genre I tried,
something new to learn or
meaningful artistic development
maybe,
pre-teen, teen, youngwoman, and,
now, woman, feeling my way
into them once again,
exploring their dustyrusty corners and
finding where they presently sit in my
throat and heart,
I had
(revolutionaryrevealing)

this thoughtinsightquestion, what?

Why are all (or so many of)
my significant songs
sungforwrittenbymadeabout
mad about
men?

What?

Okay, it's opera, so I know,
ossified and even obsolete,
old world omniscience but
where is the life and art in that?

Why in all my significant songs
are the women so
placating and personable and
silently secretly scheming, sultry
sulfur, sulphuric acid scents skin
skinned to the bone by bullshit?

My significant songs pastpresent,
taught me more about myself
than I could make mine,
at that time, but
here's a thought:

What if nowtheneverywhennow
I chose, choose, am choosing

(couldchoose)

only good songs for me?

Yearn: A verb

Yearn: a verb, an
intense feeling of
longing for
something, typically
something that one
has been lost or
separated from.

Or: to desire, to wish
very strongly, especially
for something you
cannot have or something that
is very difficult to get.

My mother tries to plant

My mother tries to plant
enough good seeds on her
heart plot in my soul to
compensate for barrens.

My mother tries to help
me understand
he's not so bad,
her point of view.

My mother tries to
two-way radio
connect us through
her airwaves but . . .

I long for a direct line
no middlemanwoman,
clean cuts,
edited, polished,
final draft,
lines aligned, and

Fuck!

Good communication,
vulnerablerealraw
only happens when
person A and B
get the message
they each meant to send,
no static interference,
ABAB form, sixteen bar return

coda, clear,
understood, understand?

(I was too young)
(he was too awkward)
(unskilled, both, he and I)
Reaching for clarity that
never came and I

I long
I long for
I long for a
I long for a direct

direct

connection.

She says (mymother)

She says (mymother),
have compassion
for my father who,
broken, broke me, and
she says he's kind and
he's listening and
he loves me, but
did he though, does he?

Did he really do all he could
as a father
toforwith me,

did he?

I have no evidence to
support that point of view.

If a father would die for

If a father would die for
his daughter,
why wouldn't he
change for her?

I'm looking for my brother

I'm looking for my brother, or
a good one fromanothermother,
because I have a vacancy
where my own brother used to be
and he's not interested
as far as I can tell
in reapplying.

I wish I remembered

I wish I remembered
it differently, good,
maybe differently, good,
like him her him, good,
fathermotherbrotherfamilytree good.
I wish I had a
catalog of good
Sears Roebuck old school
spreadsolidsizeable
instead of a pamphletleafletflyer,
less than five pages of good
memories that managed to
remain regrow robust,
even covered by lavaflowhot.
Those five were some good
memories strong, but weirdly
low bar, bare minimum
parenting, small acts of kindness.
Not yelling at knocked out teeth,
a blanket on cold night, furnace out,
a moment of watermelon popcorn summer,
breeze breezy good country tunes and cars.
Those fewfivehandfulofgoodmemories
stuck like cool roots, flowers, and
I wish I had
my memories garden full,
bursting bouquets of
genuine unconditional love, flowers,
moments, floral blossomed,
veggies rooted large like my
nanasaunties prairie summer gardens,

O!

How I wish
I remembered it

differently.

I am so tired

I am so tired
of always needing to
be compassionate,
to try,
to defend,
to chase,
to excuse,
the rude, or
have to become the
rude, to defend and

I
have
had
enough.

ENOUGH!!

He said

He said
"My door is always open," but
who cares that the door is open
when the house is always empty?

The worst part

The worst part
is the struggle
between the

hope

and the

hurt.

Sometimes

Sometimes
you have to

(youhaveto)

let go

to hold on ...

I'm dropping all my stories

I'm dropping all my stories,
like stones out of pockets, gravel, Shawshank style,
moving my dusty legs, outsteps, ankles cloudy,
uncuffing grit, bit by bit, sprinkling,
sifting, sorting, and shedding,
saltysourshorn.
All my stories, old and worn, torn up
with me at the center, unravelling the
ravelled sleeve of care and coins,
dollars paid to sew up and sweat out
dropdroopdown
the madness and melancholy of different strokes for
different folks who have maybe never heard of
or who have their own similar smallsad states of
being and resonate with pain and I,

I am
I am dropping
I am dropping all
I am dropping all my

stories,

like a shell, sure, shapedshapingshook, but
now, shoneshownsearing,
hot heat and burning up in the fire of
the belly of the beast, best,
phoenix rising ashes out and up and onandon and
I am unashamed, unshackled, and I,
(eye)
am dropping,

droppingdrop
dropdrip
dripdropdone.
Drop.
Drip.
Plunk.

At the end, plucked,
from this chapter, the
midpoint of my life,
end, ending over,

(all over, all over)

I am dropping all my stories,
I am dropping all my stories,
I am dropping all my stories,
I am dropping all my stories,
I am dropping all my stories,
I am dropping all my stories,

FREE!!!

Freeing my hands, freehandsfree to

(buildbirthbrave)

open new

(seasofsunshinerainbowsblissand)

hold

all
all the
all the new
all the new stories

I
I am
I am writing
I am writing

(writingwritingright)

now.

I want

I want
I want to
I want to GROW!

To grow, to grow and
I really can't be mad at
inadequate gardeners, because
left to my own devices
I'm a runaway species

(rampant)

and the best thing
would have been to

get the fuck out of my way,

tag along for the ride.

Not everything needs control, but

everything
needs
love.

I am unburied

I am unburied,
I am unbreathless,
I am scramblingscrounging,
tearing down, tearing up,
snotty faced, weeping, pained,
screaming, voiced, louder than loud
refusing to be unseen,
compellingconforcingconfronting

YOU MUST SEE ME!

Under this hallowed ground, confound
ringing the bell, dead undead died done
chiming chorus, o god, oh gold, oh no,
I have gone
gone so long
let you goad, grind, and grouse,
skilled skint, killed, killing me.
So long,
so longing to be with you,
connected and connecting,
all I want,

I find,

and I
am buried
(unburied) breathless
(unbreathless) bound
(unbound)
mine, my songs, my soul and I

I will sing

my songs
where they are heard,
unbury my self,
exhume, exalt,
shoutsing, and say
I am covered in glory, not dirt!
Not glory of others,
but glory of God(dess)
because HeShe blessed me, you know,
and you know,

(sometimes people destroy you)
(because they see your power and)
(frightened, don't want it to exist)

(so . . .)

my songs?

Thank god, o god, my god, goddess good, I
I have been blessed, blissed, bled,
Unburied, undone, and unwound,
(unbreathlessunbound)

My songs saved me and

I
am
no longer
screaming.

Epilogue

How did you repair that

"How did you repair that?"
she asked,

"How did you redeem that?"
she asked.

What did you do, what formula
did you follow,
what new recipetarotcarddivination
pulled you from all the
angry wreckage?

I, silenting, said,
Nothing is redeemedresolvedrepaired,
only plastered over,
replanted, potted up
in new soil and watered.
Is that redemption?
Repair?
After thirty some years
of all the unanswered questions?
The exhaustion?
Extracting, exhuming,
exfoliating, existing,
all the tiny bits
that stick
clingy
like sand and
crinkle
in your drawers and
keep you gritty instead of
smooth silk?

Sometimes they're like sandpaper,
refining all your edges and
sometimes

they rub you raw.

It's better now

It's better now
than it used to be,
but though they aren't
cruel now
(not as cruel, indifferent),
they were before and it's
strange to try to relate to
them as if they were who they are
before and now and before now.

Are they nicer because they
don't have the power to
hurtruledestroy me
anymore, or
nicer because I am stronger?

I still have to live
with the effects
of what they did and didn't and
they don'twon'tmightnever
see the effects of what they
did and didn't to me because
in the end I win,

I win.

I still have my art.
I still have my voice.
I still have myself.

I am still love and

that

can't be
so easily

silenced.

CPSIA information can be obtained
at www.ICGtesting.com
Printed in the USA
BVHW040411231122
651513BV00001BA/1